KNOW YOUR WORTH

AND ADD TAX

KALEN JOHNSON ARNOLD

Editing & Cover by Courtney Cannon at Fiction-Atlas Press.
Cover Photography by Sharon Wine at Rustic Lane Photography.

CONTENTS

INTRODUCTION

*L*et's take a walk with a cup. Think of a cup, any cup, and fill it as full or as empty as you want. Now, with your cup of water, walk around the room. There's no right way, and you have no set destination. Just walk.

Are you visualizing that cup? Is it spilling out? Did you splash any out yet? Are you walking super slow? Normal speed? Or like a Sunday stroll with no worries?

Now STOP! Who spilled their water? Did anyone else in the room spill any? How full or empty were their cups? What size cup did they have? What color? How was their speed?

You have no idea! Do you know why? For that moment, you didn't compare their life, their water, their cup size, or their spills to yours. You only cared about your cup and focusing on your own life and what your cup of water was bringing to you.

This is how you should visualize life. This is your moment. This is your time to shine. Or maybe this is your moment to sit back and truly enjoy life and stop comparing yourself to the Pinterest mom, the stay at home mom, the mom who owns a business, the mom who is a CEO, the mom who home schools her kids, moms who are tuck and rolling at drop off, the moms who look all put together, or the moms in gym clothes. Do you get where I am going?

We all compare. We all struggle just to get through this life somedays. Moms of six kids, moms of one, or moms of fur babies. We are working job(s), getting degrees, learning to find our self. The last thing we need is other ladies to judge us, mean girls—or even ourselves, pondering if we are doing enough for this life.

We all have a story. We all have good days, bad days, ugly days, sad days…but guess what? They are just that—a day. You cannot unpack and give up. This is not just a book of growth and self-help, this is a book about learning to let go. Learning that your past does not define you. Your past is just your past. Sometimes those days make you stronger and better than you ever thought you could be.

This is learning how God always has your hand and holds you through the valleys, the mountains, the highs, the lows, and the truly crappy days.

You first must know your goals and your dreams. Can you close your eyes right now? Yes, go ahead I will wait as you think about all the dreams you have. Those dreams you had as a little girl that life, chores, responsibilities, and bills all took away. Those dreams that you just knew you would have. What happened to those dreams? They change as we grow and have new dreams. I always thought I would be a teacher (I do have this degree) I do not like other kids for eight hours a day. So right now, think of your dream now. Right this moment. Is it to own a house? Go back to school? Become a nurse? Open that boutique you always thought would be fun? Be a tattoo artist? Why are you not doing these? Why are you not fighting for those dreams?

Reach down deep, light a candle, have a glass of wine, and let's learn how to dream big and let the Negative Nancy go. Let's learn to believe in yourself again.

LEARN HOW AMAZING YOU TRULY ARE

Sometimes we just need to sit down and cry. Like really. We have those days we are human and, well, we're hormonal. Some nights I sit in the bathtub and cry— not the pretty cry—the snot on your face, ugly looking like a raccoon gut-wrenching sobbing. I'm not really sure why unless I blame the stress of life, the job, being a mom and wife, but I mostly blame my depression. But really, it happens on days that my triggers hit high. I can go to the store alone and believe I am being followed, and *bam*, I am right back in the moment of being attack. I can stand in the mirror naked and start picking myself apart. These are those *I'm a busted can of biscuits* days.

I do not think you realize how much depression and anxiety take a toll on you. How much others do not see the side you hide. If you are going to see the good and how amazing life can sometimes be, you need to see the hard and ugly side of life too. If you have never felt this way, let me explain what it is like to truly get that feeling.

You feel worthless, and like everyone would be better without you. You feel like no matter how *good* you are doing, it is not enough and maybe never will be. You feel like everyone is laughing or talking behind your back. You genuinely do not feel like getting out of bed, going through the day, or even like living is doable or worth it. Depression is exhausting, and in my job, I always have to help others. I forget that sometimes I need a mental day for myself. I never realized I needed this time until one day it hit me. My mental health is just as important as my physical health. Just as yours is. We give so much to others that it can be overwhelming. So, take a break and give yourself some credit. Life is hard enough without depression and anxiety.

If you have never gone through depression or had an anxiety attack or even felt like an elephant was on your chest, then maybe this chapter is not for you, and I am a little jealous that you have never been there. But if you have, grab a blanket and sit down. Let me tell you that it will be okay.

I'm human and an anxiety-ridden lady who just can't turn her mind off. One night, with my Bud Light in hand, I looked at my naked body thinking *Girl, you got to focus! You are a trainer. You can't be in this body anymore.* Then I realized I created this body. So, I ate another cream cheese pastry and thought...*If I could take all my negative body images and work on fixing those, what might happen?*

But I must go way back to realize I was always this way.

At the early age of fifteen, I was a normal girl. Cheerleader, the baby of three girls. And was always told I was the funny one of us three. But I was not good at school. I was a good cheerleader. I was not good at taking test. I was good at talking to boys. By fifteen I had lost my virginity. Let's call him John. John was the popular guy, the football player—the fast, cool cars guy. So, I thought it was awesome that I had even gotten his attention. I still remember wearing my yellow halter top from American Eagle, my blue jean skirt that hardly covered my butt (this was cool at fifteen), and my hair just like he liked it. But after it was over, I was the normal fifteen-year-old who thought the world was ending. Don't all girls do this? Don't we all think we are so in love and finally have sex and then *bam*. You just know the world is ending and you are going to be swallowed up in the pits of hell? It cannot just be me that thought this. Two weeks later, he broke up with me and called me a whore. Now in his defense, he was a virgin before me, so I totally understood why I was being shamed and then having my name wrote on the bathroom door. I can never understand why guys can get high fives for having sex, but girls get looked down upon. But in 2001 this is how the world looked to me.

I thought I was in love. Looking back, this was my first stepping stone to learn how strong I was. This also started my eating disorder. I learned to hide not eating or I would eat enough and became a pro at throwing up. Quick, easy, and honestly, I felt like I was in control of something for the first time. By fifteen I was drawing on my body with markers, sectioning off what I thought needed to be fixed. I remember the time I did it with a permeant marker so I would see it every day and know I was not thin enough. My mom caught me, and she just had tears because she could not understand.

By eighteen I was down to 105 pounds, and you could count my ribs. But I was proud of how skinny I was, yet I looked in the mirror and still thought I was fat. I was proud I was so thin, I was proud I had gotten this small, but I was still so pissed that I was so fat. I looked in the mirror at my size two figure and all I saw was an elephant looking back at me. I was 105 pounds but felt 205.

I know back in the golden days, depression was not spoken of. We did not know how bad people were. I think a lot of it people were ashamed and thought it was weird, odd, and not normal back in the early 2000s. Thankfully, social media is opening up more discussions and it seems that people might understand it better now.

By the time high school ended, I had no clue who I was. I had no idea what I wanted to be or get out of life. I always figured God had no real purpose or calling for me. I just always felt that my life was one big joke and a mess. I would just literally 'get by' without becoming anything.

Has this, ever been you? Maybe even now, you wonder what your purpose is or what your journey is in this life. I believe we all get lost within those moments. We become a wife, mom, aunt, teacher, nurse, boss and lose *us*. You are so much more than those labels attached to your name. You are you, and you are so much more than that.

You aren't your depression.

You aren't your eating disorder.

You aren't your past.

You aren't just a mom.

You aren't your past flaws.

You aren't your regrets.

I HAD TO STOP BEING SELFISH TO REALLY LIVE

My goal was to grow up and never have kids, and well, honestly, I had no idea what I wanted to do with my life. You know, most little girls grow up wanting that family, the kids, the whole nine yards. If this was you, kudos because that means you somewhat had figured out what you wanted to do.

I wasn't that girl who had it figured out. Having depression at fifteen, I just wanted to get through each day and live.

But I tried many things. I loathed school. I truly could not stand it. I was a terrible reader and an even worse test taker. I was proud that I took the ACT four times and never passed because I could make jokes, but deep down, I felt like a loser.

I did the right thing, you know—college after high school. With a mom working for a college, I had no hopes of not going. They said no moving out till I was nineteen because heck, I didn't even have a job till I was eighteen and out of high school.

So, I did the college life. Not the partying college life, I wasn't there yet. Alcohol scared me then. I had heard the horror stories and had a cousin die because of a drunk driver, so drinking was not something I considered doing. It was all about the boys and who I was hanging out with.

So on to college and living the dream my parents had for me. After one semester of barely passing, I knew this wasn't my idea of a dream yet. At eighteen, boys and shopping were my ideas, to be honest. But I did get an associate degree and made my parents so proud. *Go me!* I thought walking across the stage—the girl who barely graduated high school because my social life and my lack of self-esteem meant I never paid attention. That girl got a two-year degree in of all things, marketing. At nineteen, I had no clue what I would even do with that degree.

As I approached the next college life, I skipped it and got married...yes, I got married, and that's a whole other chapter of another dumb thing I had to learn from. As if being married meant I could be an adult and not go to college. I could do my own things, or so I thought.

And hair school it was. I loved making people pretty and crazy colors and well, not being in college, so this was my plan. Beauty school and all my dreams would come true. Now, I did love the fact that I helped ladies feel beautiful about themselves. But the drama! Oh my, the drama! I had no idea how bad the drama would be or how competitive being a hairdresser was. I knew that there were a lot of different salons, but I am not competitive. I never have been. So, this was a whole new life for me. Then there were the drugs. Nothing too crazy, weed and some pills. But this was also new to me. Remember, I was raised in church with no dating till I was sixteen and no party life ever. So little naive me was in total shock.

This was just another stepping stone. As I finished school and learned a lot, I had a ton of melts downs. I found liquor and how I could numb the world and not even care about anything. Beauty school equaled a lot of drama. Now before a hairdresser comes at me with an axe, let me say…not ALL ladies there were drama, but geez, I didn't expect it was so competitive, and once you had a job, it was still competitive. I am not that girl. I'm the girl who plays a game to have fun. If I lose, well, okay. If I win, well, okay. So, this was a whole new life for me.

I turned to drinking, and at first, it started on Fridays and Saturdays only. We went to bars and clubs. My husband at the time, would just make it a party. As this was a new life for me, I just was there for the fun. It was fun at the time, don't get me wrong—four-inch heels, dresses as short as I could go, and as many shots as I could handle. Friday and Saturday became Thursday, then the whole week, and then I started at noon. It went from amaretto sours to margaritas to Long Island iced teas to just shots. By my twenty-second birthday, I was a pro. I could hold my liquor. I could wake up with a hangover and start drinking again because drinking helped everything.

I have friends who don't drink or just casually drink, and they even asked me why I took to drinking. Well, I honestly don't know. If you have been there, you get it. It just numbs reality, and it makes life seem easier. Maybe your outlet is working out, shopping, getting high, whatever it is. To me, this was mine.

I never really knew why I drank, but I think it was because I was so lost and empty. I was unclear at that time how miserable I was in my own head. I was lost. I was unsure of my worth, my marriage at the time was new and fun but slowly fading. I was trying to find me in liquor, and that just got me into messes and lots of broken heels from being too drunk to walk in them. Looking back, I laugh at the nights I do remember–the clubs where they knew my name and drink. The times that I don't remember, truly make me realize I was a hot mess...no I was just a mess a big ole mess.

If this has been you, laugh. I promise laughing is better than crying and saying *oh my*. It's okay. I promise we all have been young and dumb.

I always say you must have those messes to find yourself. Those messes, those lost nights, those moments of which I know I was doing wrong made me, well me. Those nights that you had dumb choices, and endless conversations or hookups, they made you, you. Right or wrong, we all have these, big or small. They shape us, so don't be so hard on yourself. Just remember you live, you learn, and you don't go back and make the same mistakes.

I was good at hiding how much I drank. I remember going to my parents with a cup, and I had been drinking. I am sure they knew, but I was the baby and I never knew when to stop. One April day, my mom told me to stop. I had a problem. I laughed at her but knew deep down I needed help. She challenged me to go out with my friends, like every weekend, and not drink. *WHAT! You want me to do what? This is not your life. I am an adult.* But this is what I did. We went to Jack's City Grill, and when they all ordered their drinks, I said water. They all laughed. I told myself I could order at the next bar. You know those moments you have the devil saying: *Just do it. Mom won't know.* This was that moment. This was the defining moment when I realized that I, at twenty-four, was an alcoholic. I will tell you that you can overcome this disease. This drug. This struggle. Do not let the numb and the darkness make your life better. I promise it hurts you more in the long run.

The day I decided I needed to be sober, that was one of those days you think: *Hey, I can do this no big deal.* I hate to say *be sober* because I did not drink all day, not all day long. I have been through that. I had stopped drinking for three years like it was nothing after a two-year binge of daily drinking. I did not realize I even had a problem at the young age of twenty-two. I thought I was just living life, like people do. Until I would drink all day long. Until I could not stop thinking about it. That's when, by twenty-four, I knew I needed to quit.

But it was easy to quit. I got pregnant with my first son. So, stopping then was easy to do. I did not pick up a drink for three years. But then I was almost thirty-three and thinking: *Why? Why do I do this to myself? Every night I start as soon as I walk through my door.*

Some days I thought I could just have one or two and half a bottle later I was like: *Whatever, I'll be better tomorrow.* Till the day tomorrow was today. So, I thought: *Let's download an app to show me the money I save, show me quotes daily, and show me that this is normal.* This is something many struggle with. We just learn to hide it.

I'm the girl that can hide things I don't want you to see. Because this is how my mind works. If they don't see it, they won't know I drink every night for three years straight. Some weekends it starts at three. I don't say this to brag I say this to tell you this is okay to admit you have a problem.

But today I quit. Today I said, enough is enough. I spend too much time, money, and my life thinking about my next drink. Sometimes I am not even sure my husband sees my struggle. He is also sober from drugs for five years now. He has been in my shoes in a different way. I think this is our biggest condition that we learn to hide from the world, the struggles that seem to make us who we truly are.

YOU ARE NOT DEFINED BY A SINGLE MOMENT

*N*ow, to continue, you must hear the good, the bad, and the ugly. The parts of life we hide. Those skeletons that you bury so deep, you hope they never escape, and are never brought up again because, well, you are ashamed and embarrassed.

This isn't a chapter that is easy to read or type. Even as I write this, the flashbacks are so real. I swore I'd keep my story hidden, but sometimes you need to share your voice.

Up until now, I have never told my full story. Why? Well, because I always felt like being raped was my fault. I somehow made it happen. I felt like I deserved it. And let me tell you, friend, if this is you right now feeling that way, you did not deserve it. You never deserve to be attacked. You never deserve to be abused. Know that this was not your fault. If you have been attacked, this chapter will be hard.

Because for those who have, we will relive it together. We understand the pain during, after, and the nightmares that come from it. If you have experienced this, my hope is that this chapter helps you let go. If you haven't been attacked, I truly hope that you understand how blessed you are.

We must first start with December 2004. I was asked to go pick up something from someone I had known for nine years. Yes, nine whole years. I had known him for so long and thought nothing was wrong with picking it up and leaving. I was nineteen, and I was naïve. Little did I know that life has a way of showing you just how much you can trust people. My life would never be the same after this day.

I walked into the house. It was a home I had been in many times. I'd had dinner with his parents, swam in the pool, and had even gone to church with this person. The stairs were right through the front door. You could see his bedroom from the doorway. He smiled like normal, and we did the usual odd hug. Then he told me the thing I had come to pick up was upstairs.

This should have been my red flag, but you know those friends you know like the back of your hand and think nothing of it? Yes, it was that friend. As we walked into his room, he shut the door. Again, at nineteen, you don't think anything is wrong. He locked the door and pushed me down. I told him I needed to leave, and he took my keys and threw them across the room. They hit his wall by his bathroom and fell to the floor. I froze. I did not know what was going on until my underwear was pulled down and my hands were held over my head. At that moment, at that exact moment, I wanted to die. He was so heavy and his breath was so hot. All I remember was trying to kick him and make him stop. I wanted to literally just lay there and die. I fought, but I was a hundred and five pounds of nothing but bones. I was lying there crying having a panic attack, my very first panic attack.

I did not understand why he was doing this to me. When he was done, I grabbed my keys and ran out the door. I got in my car, and I cried for the whole ten minutes home.

I told no one. I told myself it was my fault. I told myself that I deserved it. I told myself that I was worthless, and it was because I did something wrong.

That was the worst moment of my life up until then. I went home and showered and cried and scrubbed my body. I needed to wash it off of me. Wash that unwanted sex from my body. Wash the fact that I had no idea what I had just gone through. I had no idea I was even raped. I had no idea what had happened. I couldn't sleep. I couldn't eat, and my parents had no idea.

It took me until February to admit what happened to my mom. I left church early to go home and kill myself, and she begged me to tell her who and I refused to. I could not do that. I would ruin him and his family. Again, I was nineteen and dumb. I thought this was the worst day. I felt I deserved it. And I thought I would be defined as a rape victim.

This was when therapy started for me. I began attending sessions two times a week, and my parents had to hide all the knives, guns, pills—anything I could use to harm myself. At that time, I had no idea how bad I was or that being raped was wrong. Even in therapy, I downplayed how it made me feel. I thought they would think I put myself in the situation. Or that I deserved it also.

We continued to go to the same church, and I avoided him like a mouse. I could not even look at him. One Sunday night, I was going out the door as he came in, and we smacked into each other. I looked at him, and I told him I forgave him for what he did. He smirked and said, okay. He gave me this look like I was a complete idiot. I look back now and can laugh at that moment. I wanted I hide. I thought forgiving him would make it leave my mind. Like forgiving him would make the tears stop, and the night terrors disappear. Maybe that did not happen, but I needed to forgive him in order to release this anger. I needed to forgive him so I could forgive myself.

Skip to April 2011, when I thought I was a normal twenty-six-year-old with a background that was hidden enough that it would never be brought back up. A past that was so rough, that if I told anyone, they would never understand.

By this time, I was married and had been for five years. I

had a one-year-old son. My marriage was ending. I was alone. I hated the world.

When this rape started, I think the thought of this person, of all people, doing this is what stuck with me.

This person knew. This person knew the damage it caused me. This person was my rock many times. And this person put me through hell for the longest forty minutes of my life.

So many times, I pass that dang white house and think: *Today I'll have no flashbacks. Today I'll just see a normal, pretty, white farmhouse and think nothing of it.*

For three years, this was my house. It was a beautiful old farmhouse with a swing and cows surrounding it. The kind of house you see in movies and think: *If that house could talk.* During those three years, this house held parties, family dinners, and many memories that still, years later, make me cry.

It was the week of Easter. I remember trying to find the right outfit for my son. Finding a dress that would fit and be a 'Mom' dress. I had finally gotten my drinking under control and hadn't had a drink in almost three years or more. I was a mom now, and focusing on my son was all that mattered.

My marriage was ending, and here I was with a one-year-old. I was getting ready to go back to school in the Fall, trying to pick up the pieces and trying to find myself while doing all of this. That's when I realized the joke. I was a single mom who had never lived on her own ever and who was in school and making ends meet as a bartender.

It was April 2011 and raining. It was one of those days you try blacking out, yet you can't no matter how many times you try. It was a day I would relive for years to come, but a day that I knew I had a child to fight for.

I was packing up mine and my son's stuff to move out. I was a mess. I knew it was time but at twenty-six, let's be honest, I didn't expect I'd be filing for divorce. I did not expect to be standing there with a guy I had known for seven years and have him shove me onto my own bed. I never thought I would be standing face to face with him telling me I couldn't leave. The next forty minutes, I remember every detail—every look he gave me, every smirk I got. And his voice still haunts me saying: *You know you want this.*

Next thing I knew I was being thrown onto my bed. I was held down, and my clothes were ripped off. At first, I was in total shock and disbelief that this was happening AGAIN.

In my mind, up to this point, I had already lived through it once, and I did not expect to live through it again.

As it happened, and the rape began, I told myself: *Last time you didn't fight... Today it won't define you.* Looking back, I know I fought with all my might this time. I was scared. I yelled. I'm not sure how many times, but I know that if anyone were close, they would have called the cops. I cried. And then there was the look in his eye when he winked at me and said: *I know you want this.* And I finally just gave up because I knew I wasn't strong enough. I closed my eyes and cried, and this was the longest forty minutes of my life.

He felt like five hundred pounds. He felt like he was crushing the life out of me, and I could not even breathe with him on top of me. I felt I was being crunched with every move. I remember hearing the clock tick, tick, tick, tick. After it was over, it was like he snapped out of whatever daze he was in and kept apologizing to me. He kept assuring me he did not mean to do it. He did not know what came over him. Did I believe him? No, and I still don't. It took me four years to forgive him, and I still can't look at him if I see him out somewhere.

This day was the day I realized I was more than just a girl fighting to stay alive. I was a girl who would not let anything stop me. This was the day that as it unfolded, and as it started and ended...I grabbed my stuff and ran and drove. How I got to my son and then got to my safe place and cried, I have no idea.

I remember sitting with a friend and crying for hours thinking: *How could I let this happen to me again? I'm stronger than that. I'm worth more than being raped twice now.* The words I heard stayed with me.... this wasn't your fault, and no one deserves it ever. Do not let this define you.

Up until that day, I have never thought of it that way. *It-wasn't-my-fault.* Four simple words that changed my whole outlook. This wasn't my fault.

You see, in that moment of weakness, of doubt, of I have nothing but a one-year-old, that I had just stared at, I had someone finally tell me I was worth more than having someone putting me through that.

As you read those words, you are worth more than a label. Whether it be rape, assault, emotional abuse, none are worse than the other. How do I know? I have been in a relationship with all three. I honestly always say I would rather you hit me then mentally abuse me. Why? The bruises heal, and I can handle them. The words, once spoken, no matter if it was years ago, last month, or yesterday, they stay with you. Those words that have been said to you—be it by family, friends, a bully, or a parent—they will stay with you and haunt you.

Rape is nothing that you did. The first time, I was in what I thought was a friend's house and the other, in my own home with someone who had a key. We have been told to hide it, not speak of it. To never let anyone know how bad it was. To fight. And the worst thing is, we are told it is our fault. We should not have been at the party. We should not have put ourselves in that situation. We should have known better. Guess what, beautiful lady, I promise you that if you have been there, you did not deserve it, and you are worth more than being defined by your rape. You are worth more than being told you know you want it. You are worth more than someone not listening when you say no. Never, I mean never, let that moment define you. You are a person.

No matter if you are at a party. No matter if you are with a friend. No matter if you had a few drinks. No matter if you had none. Rape is not okay. Rape is not your fault. I am here to tell you today, at the moment you read this, that you did nothing wrong. You did not deserve it. You did not deserve to be held down. I am here to tell you to wipe those tears, just like I am, and look in the mirror and tell yourself that you are strong, brave, and beautiful.

THE UNEXPECTED

*I*n November of 2008, my world got turned upside down and flipped around. My mom was supposed to be having a normal everyday surgery. Around lunchtime, my dad texted my sisters and me. The text read: *Your mom has cancer. She does not know. And I know no more.*

If you have lost someone or watched someone go through chemo, saw the sickness, I want to hug you. This was one of the hardest moments of my life—watching my mom change before my eyes, not just physically but mentally.

And those words would shake my family for the next nine months. For the next nine months, I would shave my mom's head. I would wear pink like it was my life. I would cry more than I admitted.

The chemo took my mom away—my fun mom, who was

my friend. The chemo made her body so frail and so weak. I would make her lunch and tell her it would be okay as I held her with tears running down my face.

One day I went to fix her soup and she was lying on the kitchen floor crying over her spilled chicken noodle soup. She was too weak to stand and too stubborn to wait on me, but this was the moment I knew my mom needed me. This is a picture I have in my mind, but I got her up, cleaned her off, and we once again sat on the couch, and I held her like she used to hold me, and still does, and I said: *This will be okay.* Little did I know that next thing that would happen. Pregnancy.

December 1st, 2008, I found out I was pregnant, and I cried because I could not be a mom. This wasn't the life I plan. I was not going to be a mom. Remember, this was not my idea of life or what I wanted to do. I was mad at God. I won't even lie to you. I was so mad, I had a mom with cancer, and now I had a baby in my belly and I never even wanted that.

Little did I know that in the next few weeks of my life, I would learn what family and faith really were.

THE CHILD THAT TAUGHT ME WHAT LIFE IS ABOUT

I did not want this child I was having. I know that is hard to read. But I was selfish. I was on my own time, not wanting to be a mom. I know that seems so mean and wrong. But I am laying it out there. I think of the ladies I have met who would do anything for a baby and, at that moment, looking back how terribly selfish I was. But you know some people just do not want to be a mom, and well, currently, I was that person.

By twelve weeks in, I was excited. I had begun understanding how exciting being a mom was and was already planning names. Jan 26th was a Friday, and I went in for an ultrasound at twelve weeks and three days. I was alone just a checkup what could go wrong? I sat and waited and waited. They called my name back, and they went to hear the heartbeat and nothing. They assured me that it was nothing they would get another doctor to come in and see me. I texted my mom because, well, she is supposed to fix everything. She told me to be calm, and she was on her way. As I laid there waiting, I just prayed that God to let the baby be okay. I knew I was not excited, but I did not want anything bad to happen. As the doctor came in, he looked for a heartbeat and said: *Ma'am, you lost your baby at nine weeks and five days.* He wiped my belly off and told me to wait for an appointment for D&C. The moment is embedded in my mind. I still see him there with no emotion just: *That's it. Your body was not ready*—nothing else.

That was it. I was just lying there alone, tears coming down, and he just said it happens. Now I get this, it happens, but that was my baby. This is so many ladies lying on the bed, wiping tears for their baby. This is reality for so many who have been in my shoes and for you right now reading this. Know that I type this and wipe my tears for you and myself. I am holding you telling you I know exactly what you feel. One day we will meet our babies again, and this is what I cling to on those days I wish I could hold my baby.

Due to it being a Friday afternoon, they could not do surgery until Monday. This was the longest weekend ever. I cried and cried and cried. I yelled at God. I yelled at him for me not wanting this baby, and then when I accepted it, he took that precious baby from me.

Monday, January 29th, I went to the hospital for the D&C. My mom had her pre-op for her cancer removal on Thursday, so she came and hugged me and left. I cried. I begged them to let me see my baby. I begged them to let me just hold it. I never knew how even nine years later, I would be so affected still. One day I'll see my baby, and I truly believe it was my little girl I so long to have. Her name would have been Karrington. She would have been so loved.

The nurse who came in before and prayed for me wiped my tears told me this: *Know that you are chosen by God because you are strong. You are special.* Even though the tears would not stop that day, a piece of my heart was taken.

On February 1st, after three days of pain. I ended up in the ER due to blood loss and clots. I have to say how scared I was and again. I called my parents, but it was 2 AM. The doctor told me I had too much scar tissue, and to ever get pregnant again would be a blessing. That my chances just went down because my body hates me is what I thought. They gave me medicine and sent me home.

By eight in the morning, I was back at the hospital, this time for my mom.

I was sitting surrounded by family and friends waiting on my mom to come out of surgery. Cancer sucks. There is no nice way to say it. There is no way of saying it nicely. This was my mom. She was young, and she was not supposed to have cancer or have a chance to leave my family. She came out, and they told us they got it all and sent her home the next day. But cancer does not just affect the person who has it. Our whole family's lives changed—from us taking her to treatment, me shaving her head, seeing her strong body get weak, to seeing her faith grow, and her still being the rock of our family. She fought and had chemo weekly.

On April 23rd, we had a huge party and kicked cancer's butt. As I saw her smiling and her bald head just as shiny and smooth, I saw my mom in a different light. So many times, she saved me. She and my dad were my rock during this time. We all had to be strong for her. I cried a lot, but never in front of her. I prayed and beg God to not take her. But at this moment, I can still see her and how blessed she knew she was. She is a warrior.

I found out on July 4th, 2009, that I was pregnant. This was the happiest day. I was thrilled. This little boy, a year later, would save my life in ways he will never know. He gave me life and taught me what real love was.

My outlook changed. I realized that I had a little human I was responsible for. Being a mom changes you. It changes how you do everything. Never forget even if you are not a mom, someone needs you. Someone is watching you and proud of you.

I am proud of you. If it is all you realize during this book, know you are needed. Know there are people watching you and praying for you. There are people wanting to see you do better than the day before. There are people waiting for you to reach those dreams and create bigger ones. There are people who are clapping for you, and you have no idea. And lastly, you are inspiring someone just by being strong and living this life.

I always believe that even if someone is waiting to see you fail, someone else is secretly cheering for you and waiting for you to truly do exactly what God called you for. Someone you do not even know is waiting for you to say: *I did it.* And guess what, you will do it and so much more. Keep fighting daily, beautiful lady.

YOU ARE WORTH IT

March 2005 was my first attempt at killing myself. I never really knew at the time why. Maybe because I had not told anyone I had been raped. Maybe because I had no idea I was even depressed and was living a life that as a Christian, I knew was so wrong. I was once again letting a guy in, and once again, he hurt me. He ripped my heart out. This was that guy that I had known since I was in elementary school, and we went to church together. We dated a few months. He had no idea about my past. But he was so kind, caring, adorable, and honestly treated me better than anyone had thus far, which was not saying a lot.

Valentine's day 2005, we had just broken up, and he asked to see me after work. I was a waitress and I knew it would be late and my parents wouldn't think anything. So, I said sure. We meet in a bowling alley parking lot. Chatted for a few minutes, and yes, messed around. He then told me to get out and never text him again. This was the moment that I knew what true heartbreak was. I had no idea that people were this crappy. I was already at my lowest. Fighting demons, I had no idea that even existed and this guy I was so in love with just told me to never text him after using me. Now, if you have never had this happen, I high five you because I was so easily used. Yes, I just admitted this. But if you have been there, I hug you big right now if this is bringing those random nights up, that make you want to scream and maybe punch someone.

So here I was sitting in my driveway at 2 AM thinking just drive off a bridge and just end this hurt. Just drive so fast that you can just die. This moment is still so clear. And for some reason, my mom texted me: *Where are you?* This is the first time my mom saved me. This is the moment that defines my life. Because at 2 AM I was ready. I was sitting in my tan 1997 Honda Accord, believing that driving off a bridge was the best choice I had for the life I was leading and the emotions I was feeling.

This was a whole new thing for me. I get asked why I felt that way, why just ending my life seemed easier than facing it head-on.

If you have felt these thoughts, friend, I know it all too well. I proudly have my semicolon tattoo, knowing my story could have ended many times, but God had bigger plans for me. He has bigger plans for you. He has us, and he understands, even if sometimes we do not understand why we feel this way.

Sometimes the thoughts are so strong. Sometimes you cannot get out of your own head. The thing with depression or any mental illness is that you aren't in the right mindset. You aren't in the right mind frame to understand. Those feelings of not being needed or good enough for anyone are just so strong. Sometimes no one seems to understand. And guess what? This is okay because you are not alone. You will never be alone. So many face this daily. Suicide is something that, sadly, is happening every day around us. It is something that is close to home for many people that I see. I always get asked why you can't just get off that low. Well, if I could just snap out of it, trust me, I would and guess what so many others would too. I think somedays we forget to check on those who are always positive. Those who are smiling, happy, and helping other people. Those individuals normally hold the deepest hurt and struggles. Not many see my struggles daily because I don't want to be defined by my mental health. I want to be known as someone who helps ladies find their worth. Do I cry more than I admit? Yes. I even think my closest friends know me better than myself. They check on me on the days I need them to, and they don't even know it.

So often, doctors and therapists push pills. Push you to just talk, and sadly, so many times, the words aren't there to talk. The thoughts that run through people's head during these lows are controlling.

2005 was a defining year of hitting rock bottom while being a college student and thinking I could have a 'normal' life while hiding an eating disorder and depression—all while smiling and telling everyone I was fine.

Is this you? Do you understand that you aren't alone and that so many people are in your shoes? Those days you just need a hug, and no one is there to give you one. Those days you sit on the bathroom floor crying for whatever trigger hit you today. Those days that you look in the mirror and truly just cry because a busted can of biscuits happen to you. You will never be alone. And for me knowing this and knowing that God will not give me more than I can handle even if I question him a lot about his will, comforts me. I do know that there is a reason we have our battles. There is a reason we have highs and lows. There are reasons we go through the valley and somedays we don't think we can climb that mountain. Do not stop climbing. Do not give up on yourself.

By the time 2006 rolled around, my mom had picked me up off the floor in full-blown depression just to try to help me make it through the day. Laying in bed sleeping and crying was so much easier than facing the world, the hurt, the thoughts. Mom had to leave work or take off many times because I could not be left alone. It was one of the last times I tried to kill myself, and my mom once again saved me. I had written letters to my sisters and to my parents explaining they did not need my burden anymore. That they needed me out of the family. This time my therapist told me I needed to either learn to control it or I would be put in the nuthouse. This was one of the moments I needed to see I was not 'fixable.'

After my first marriage came to an end, I realized how bad I truly was as I stood with a one-year-old on my own for the first time ever. I just sat and held him and cried. I just looked at him in our own townhouse thinking: *How I am going to make it and not hit bottom again?* This was the bottom I needed to rebuild the Kalen I am today.

I finally accepted in 2014 that I needed more help than I would admit. This was after a second kid, another marriage, and a husband who finally got how bad I was. He handled me and still does better than anyone ever has.

And I went to a doctor and started on Zoloft for the first time. If you have ever taken it, it is amazing. I had no emotions. I had no cares, no worries, and I was fat and happy as I look back on it because nothing mattered to me.

By 2017 I had been through five pills, and many had

made me worse. Each time we changed medication only for it to not work or stop working a new low would come over me. A new moment of suicidal thoughts would raise up. Each moment I couldn't be left alone, my parents would keep the boys, and I would lay on their couch and just not move. I'm pretty sure I have the best parents who knew exactly how bad I was and who never questioned helping me.

My husband had never gone through anything like this until me. Some days he still does not understand depression, but he is there. He holds me. He allows me just to go sit alone when it's a bad day, and he doesn't question me. He understands that somedays, I cannot go to the store with two kids, or even go alone. Sometimes I look over my shoulder ten times and leave without anything because I cannot make it without an anxiety attack. I am blessed to have the support I do. If you don't have that, find it. Find that person who understands and just listens or just hugs you. Sometimes you just need five minutes alone to know that it's okay to not be okay. But don't you unpack and quit fighting. You are a survivor. You are doing amazing. You have survived how many bad days? How many lows? And you're still fighting to keep being a better you. You have a story, don't you dare hide from the amazing person you are.

Never forget you aren't alone. Since then, I have changed again, and I decided to try CBD oils and to do it my own way. Not a doctor's way. Not a therapist's way. The way that my body will let me be me, not drowning in a fog separated from life. To be more present and not stuck in my own head. Never feel like depression makes you weak, or that anxiety makes you worthless. This is not your fault. I have learned and accepted that I was born with this. I have a past that, yes, at times, made it worse but made me stronger. A past that made me who I am. I hate when I hear 'if this hadn't happened, I wouldn't have been through this.'

If all the trauma I've been through in my life did not happen, I'd never have found how strong I really am.

I wouldn't have a story to help others know it is okay. You are not worthless. You are not useless. You are amazing. You are strong. And you have been to hell and are still standing because God has a plan.

Ladies, we are our own worst critic. Let's be honest. We can tear ourselves apart while building others up. We can tell someone they are beautiful and look in the mirror and think: *Why are you so plain? Ugly? Not attractive? Boring?*

You see, this is where you have to step up and realize you are not like that girl.

Wait, I'm supposed to be building you up, not telling you that you are not like those girls, right?

But you aren't.

You, my friend, are a superhero all on your own because you are the only you there is.

You are the only you that is made just like you.

You are the only beautiful you.

You are the only amazing you.

Don't crave more. Don't lust for me.

Accept your flaws. Accepts your actions and be you.

THERE IS ONLY ONE YOU AND YOU
ARE PERFECTLY MADE

*D*o you get on social media and just get depressed?
Well, I guess not depressed, but annoyed by these
ladies' bodies who look, well, perfect? Way before social
media, this was magazines for me. I hated those girls I did
not even know. I hated those prom books of perfectly skinny
girls when I went to find my prom dresses.

I think an eating disorder can develop for many reasons. I
have had different people walk through my doors over the
years. Some do it because they hate themselves. Some
because they were raised in a house where being fat was
looked down upon. My reason was a control thing. I felt like
I had no control over anything in my life besides my size.
That sounds so crazy now as I type this. But it's honestly
how I was and still am.

How many times have you set behind a computer screen

or a phone screen and questioned your worth? Questioned if you are good enough? Compared yourself to people you know? People you have never meet and never will? How many times have you gone from feeling amazing and proud of your accomplishments to feeling like a busted can of biscuits?

Yesterday I unfollowed 400 people. Why? They won't even notice, but guess what? I noticed that I was comparing myself, my job, my year, and my body. We all do this. Even if you don't notice it, you probably are.

At fifteen, I started the let's-skip-a-meal behavior. Skipping a meal went from two meals, to let's just eat when I have to and force myself to throw up. Now, if you hate to throw up, this method would never be for you. I did it for so long I can throw up with no struggles. Again, I giggle, but in my fifteen-year-old mind, I was controlling my body that I would one day love. I don't think then, or even now, I realized how messed up my idea of this was. I reasoned with myself daily that it would be okay. Once I started working, I went to diet pills. I would take different ones throughout the day, and how I did not kill myself, I do not know.

I do not think we decide as ladies or humans to starve ourselves, but social media and the world sucks and makes you believe if you aren't a certain size, you will never make it. You won't get that job, that guy, that house, that money. And please tell me in what reality is any of this real?

By twenty, I was so good at this not eating life that I was a stick. I look like I had done drugs my face was so sunken in. I look now and am truly disgusted. Not because of who I was, but that my mind was so messed up that I looked like a breathing skeleton and I thought that was okay. But quitting was not easy. I went to therapy for this. I went to prayer meetings for it. I would journal thinking it would help. But honestly, I could not stop. It seems simple if you have never struggled with this. Just eat, dang it. But to someone who does this, I know the struggles are all too real. Those diet pills seem easy. You look in the mirror at 120 pounds, and you swear you look 220 pounds. But let me tell you, beautiful, you are a size awesome and perfect the way you are. Work daily on realizing this.

It took me meeting my second husband to truly get control. At twenty-eight, I was still starving myself and was teaching five cardio classes a week. I would blackout, and I would almost pass out. I know one night I just had to stop teaching, and I genuinely was scared for my life. Because when I had a class of fifty-plus, I could not be that 'fat trainer' they expected more from me. When in reality, they did not expect anything but me. I was the one expecting too much from myself.

Fall Break October 2015, we were at the beach and went to a family-owned ice cream parlor. I'd had my second son already and was 130 pounds. I ate my normal brownie sundae and went to go throw up, and my husband told me no. I was so mad at him. He took my hand, and he said: *I will not let you keep doing this to yourself.* That moment someone told me to stop. Sure, many had up to this day, but none who truly was there watching me. He saw me nightly push food around, so I looked like I ate. He saw me run to the bathroom before I couldn't get it all back up. This was my defining moment of my eating disorder. This was the moment that I needed to know someone needed me to stop and love myself. Maybe, therefore, I have a passion for fitness like I do. Perhaps this is the reason I have the job I do.

If this is you starving, not eating, or simply throwing up, I beg you to stop and look in the mirror. If you could see yourself through the eyes of those who love you. If you could take off your blinders and stop tearing yourself apart, you would find you are worth so much more then killing yourself from the inside out. You are beautiful and made perfectly. You have flaws, we all do. Some just hide theirs better than others. Some have Botox and so many injections. The prettiest faces can have the ugliest personalities and tell the most horrid lies. The girl that doesn't believe she is pretty enough is the funniest, the secret keeper.

Looks fade, the body changes. But, beautiful lady, you are amazing! Accept those moments, those stretch marks, those flaws because they made you beautiful.

YOU KNOW YOUR KIDS BETTER THAN ANYONE

*T*here are those days that you fuss at your kids not because they are doing anything wrong, they simply just need help. This was one of those days. My son asked for lunch. No biggie, right? But when you have been up all night with an elephant on your chest and fighting back the urge to puke, it's not just a lunch. As I fussed that he could not just warm up a piece of pizza, it hit me. I was a terrible person. It wasn't just warming up the lunch. It was so much more than that. It was the fact that, at that moment, I couldn't just be a mom because I was fighting an anxiety attack. I sat in my living room just crying. He had no clue I even was crying. About twenty minutes later, I yelled for him to finish up and come see me.

At this moment, I saw everything I was fighting for, and I just knew this was the moment and time I knew he understood I was struggling and fighting to gain control. As I hugged him and apologized for the yelling and for simply not making his lunch, I realized at eight that he got it. I realized he understood that I was having a moment of self-doubt in the world. I was having a moment of insecurity that I even could do this.

As moms, I believe we question a lot of our worth in how we raise our kids. You know mom's joke saying: *If you hear me yelling, just ignore it!* to the neighbors. But in all honestly, my eight-year-old understood. He knows I take medicine to help me daily. He told me once he was glad, I don't yell and cry like I used to. He knows when I need a hug more than anyone does. We have that connection. We have this bond from three years just being us and truly me fighting to keep food on the table and wondering how I would buy diapers and everything for a one-year-old. We have a bond that is unbreakable. Moms, as you are reading this, know you are doing the best you can. No matter if you have support or you are making it alone. Maybe you cannot do the fancy Disney trips or beach trips, but you can love that baby more than anyone can. You are the mom, and that is the most special blessing you can have. But don't forget you are human. Don't forget we all make mistakes. We all yell and raise our voices. We all have those moments of self-doubt and believe others are better at the mom-life then we are. And if you aren't a mom yet, or chose not to be one, I genuinely want to hug you right now because that itself is hard to decide.

Three years ago, in kindergarten, my son was suffering from some things himself. He was me. He was fighting something he nor anyone else really could understand. He was fighting something that at first, even I could not understand. It took me weeks of bitten shirts and principal's office visits for me to see my son was slowly becoming me. He was fighting something he did not understand at the age of six. He was fighting something and would black out and not understand why. He would fight me, kick me, and just yell at me. I would cry. I would yell.

We had so many tests ran—scans done on his little brain to make sure the headaches weren't causing the blackouts. The bitten shirts that he ruined so many of with holes were because he was stressing out so badly and had no idea what was wrong.

I would fight back because I had no idea that he was fighting me because he was having a panic attack. It took me a few weeks to see he needed more help than I could give him after the doctor finally looked at me and said he really needs therapy, not more tests. After seeing a therapist and realizing he was a mini-me, I realized he didn't understand at six what was going on. After seeing that a therapist did not know how to control his thoughts, his anger, his frustration, I saw I could help. I had been here before.

Finding his triggers worked wonders. Finding his outlet was like a whole new miracle. But I got hell for putting him into therapy. I was told I didn't know how to be a mom if I had to take a six-year-old to therapy instead of spanking him or fussing at him. There is a big difference in his behavior and that of an unruly child. He didn't know what he was going through. He did not understand the problems he was having. He just knew that he blacked out and was mad—at what, he did not know. Maybe because his parents divorced at one. Maybe because his mom had let him down. Maybe because his parents had both remarried. At six, life is totally different, and I was willing to help any way I could if he would not end up having the same problems I had, even if that meant I got looked down upon as a mother.

It has been three long years, and so many things have changed for him. He has OCD and needs schedules, and we make it work. Therapy is as needed, and we let him draw anytime he needs an outlet. You see, if I had listened to those typical medical options, my son might not be where he is today. If I had listened to the whispers of you cannot just help your son, I would not have the kid I have today.

So, moms, you know you kid better than anyone, you know their hearts and their thoughts. It's okay to help them and do things others do not agree with. Because guess what? Those professionals and whisperers do not pay your bills, nor do they have to live with the consequences.

LEARNING YOUR WORTH

*W*ork. Blah. Ever had a job you hated. Like dreaded waking up and going to? This was me at eighteen. My first job was retail. I can't do it. I won't lie. I have no filter I wanted to tell them: *No, that doesn't look good.* And I was eighteen. Need I say more? It was so bad. I never did retail again.

Your hope is that you like your job. You hope you have a job that brings you joy. My job is one that is amazing. I love my job. My job is rewarding. I don't just like my job. I would work free. I genuinely love seeing people who find their worth, who find confidence. This is a passion. This is not just a job.

It wasn't always this way. I have been the broke bartender who made drinks for those who wouldn't stop talking to me. I have waited tables for many who look down on me. I was a substitute teacher for kids that were brats.

I have had a boss that made me question my worth—my ability. I think we all have those co-workers or bosses. We have those who make you feel like you're a puppet on a string just doing what they believe is best for you, but in reality, you're doing what is best for them. We have those jobs that start off fantastic, and then you see the light and the truth. Even if you meet amazing people those jobs and those moments stay with you. We are human. If you don't question your worth once a week, are we really being honest with ourselves? But should a job or a person truly make you feel like you are uneducated and worthless? If you have been there or are there now, leave because you will feel so much better. I was there, I was the one that had no idea how much I was being used until my true friends said: *Kalen, leave. It's your time to shine.* Those moments, those friends who I say are true and who are loyal and real, they are why I am here. They are why I am writing this book. Because they told me to try it. So here I am typing away, looking at my Christmas tree and reliving moments that I have buried so deep that I cry as I type. I have to take a step back and take deep breaths. And I have days I don't even open my laptop because the triggers are so real. But as I sit here and relive moments, know that this one is real. I was bullied as an adult. I was used by a mean girl. I questioned my worth, my job, my ability, my marriage—and I questioned if I should even try to keep going on all because of one person. Shew, that was deep. Re-read that. Yes, go back and read it. If this is you in friendship, marriage, family, job, anything, walk away with your head held high and know you are better and worth more than being a puppet.

As you enter into life and start seeing changes and maybe lose people, you learn that you are receiving a lesson, or maybe, it's a blessing that God took out the trash. Funny to say that, but I had a friend tell me that one day and it stuck with me. Allow God to take the trash out—to take those relationships, people, jobs, situations—let him take them out and truly learn what lesson he is trying to teach you. Now, I never said that this was easy because even if it's a simple friendship, sometimes it hurts to the core. Maybe it's a loved one who you had to walk away from, a job, a career. There are so many times that God is there and takes care of a situation you thought would break you. Guess what? If it did break you, you are so much stronger because of it. You are stronger and know so much more because of that situation. Don't you dare sit and ponder why. I promise it will be shown sooner or later why he removes people from your life. But during that moment, I pray you feel at peace. I hope you see your worth during those moments. You can cry, but unpacking and staying there being a Debbie downer is not allowed.

I had a friend going through a divorce, and I had heard

why all from them. And the more I listened the more I wanted to scream you don't know your worth! It was not because they were better without their spouse, it was simply that he did not know his worth at that moment. After moments of tears and hard times, I finally asked him if he knew his worth, truly knew it. Maybe this is you in a situation. Why tolerate someone who belittles you, puts you down, or makes you feel not good enough. Why put up with that?

In my job, I see ladies of all backgrounds. I get to know ladies. Their past, their marriages, I know their bad days, I see their stress, and sometimes I even know way more than I need to. I know more about these ladies than their best friend, their boyfriend, their husbands. When they come and start losing weight, they start being open. You see, you gain weight because of many reasons. I must get to the reasons why. I believe that many times this is how ladies find their worth. So many times, I have seen them hit their lowest right there in front of me, opening up and realizing why they gain weight. My joke is when I make you cry, it means I broke you, and we build you back from there.

Weekly ladies cry, not from working out but from life. From holding it together in front of everyone, and they see me, and I guess I make them cry.

So many tell me how they hurt. Some tell me how their

husbands emotionally abuse them. I have helped ladies leave their abusive husbands. Some ladies I teach to let go and just enjoy being single and young. The best moments are those who say they need help to feel sexy and to know that their body is amazing. You see, when a lady can learn that her body is a beautiful thing, flaws and all, is when you know you have reached that point where you are not just their trainer. Sometimes I read texts and think: *Did you just really ask me this?* From them setting up sexy pictures for their husband to walking out of the dressing room in their sports bra showing me how proud they are of the weight they lost. I see it all. I love the ladies who come in and say I told that guy he never answered, and I was worth more than not answering my texts for five days. Those moments they come and tell you they see their toes after years of being over 250 pounds. They become so much more aware of how beautiful they are inside and out.

Sometimes you must remember these girls were just like me, bullied, no self-esteem, gaining weight, losing weight, losing their self-worth, and they have a past they don't want others to know about. These are the moments I realize I have a past just like them. We are all human.

We all have things we think if others knew they would never understand. The moment you realize that you are worth taking that hike, taking time to read that book, work on that podcast, start that business, or climbing that corporate ladder, you know you found your worth.

These ladies do not realize when they walk into my

studio that it is not just about fitness; they learn about their worth. They learn how amazing they are. How beautiful they are not just on the outside, but inside as well. As ladies walk in the doors, you learn how strong you are. You must step out of a box.

You see, when you find your worth, when you realize how amazing you truly are, how beautiful you are, things change. Things will start looking brighter. Things will start to unfold, and you start seeing life differently.

You must stand up for yourself. You allow what you put up with. If someone is belittling you, stop allowing it. Stop allowing someone to steal your joy. Stop allowing someone to take a job you know you worked for. Speak up. Speak up when you are being a doormat for others. Speak up. You have a voice. Your voice is loud, use it. Don't allow someone to use you, make you a puppet, or think you are beneath them

YOU ARE SO MUCH MORE.

GOD DOESN'T PROMISE FAIRY TALES AND RAINBOWS EACH DAY

*W*e grow up watching wonderful Disney movies and expect life, love, relationships, friendships, everything to be just happy daily with no problems. We expect life to be, well, a fairy tale.

Have you really ever thought about how God allows every high and low? Every mountain and valley, every door open and closed for a lesson and a blessing. God takes the trash out when he knows you are beyond needing that toxic relationship. God takes the trash out when you have outgrown that lesson when you are ready for the next blessing. When you are ready to grow and get your wings, and this is exactly when you have to have faith that you are exactly where God wants you to be.

Think of a moment a time that you prayed for an answer

or a situation and got nothing. God did not answer. Or God wasn't giving you the answer you wanted. Or better yet, you weren't listening because you did not like the answer. We do this in every situation, marriage, jobs, friendships those moments we come and say you aren't okay, and they explain, we run.

STOP RUNNING.

Stop allowing a door that is open to be slowly closing in your face just to sit in the hall and want to bang on that door. When that friend walks away, let them. When that friend uses you, realize you aren't a doormat. When that job is not going anywhere, and you are miserable, change it. Find another one. When that marriage is failing, fix it.

STOP RUNNING.

Stop allowing your own thoughts and struggles to be the reason you do not hear God when he is loudly telling you the answer, even if it is not the answer you want to hear. Wait in the hallway and dance, cry, scream, yell, pray, but never think this is the end of that road. Never think this is the moment it ends. Be ready for the next chapter of your life.

No, life is not rainbows and butterflies, but guess what? It is so much more, better, and bigger than the fairy tales. So many times, people throw in the towel and give up easily. I see this every day in my own studio and in my own life. I see ladies saying the weight isn't coming off fast enough or where they wanted it, so they throw in the towel and give up after a month. Now let's be honest you can't lose thirty plus pounds in a month, and it be healthy. But guess what? You can keep fighting, keep pushing, keep getting stronger, and give it three months and be proud of yourself for not quitting.

As I have spoken to a friend lately, we have discussed how people just run when things get hard. We run when things seem to be too hard to wade through, instead of having faith and being strong and leaning on God for our strength and to be our rock. I think in life as we are willing to quit, it shows how we don't have the faith that we say we do. If we are willing to quit so easily when it is hard, why would God allow us to arrive at the mountain so we can praise him when we quit instead of trusting him. During those moments of lows and trials, praise Jesus. During those moments of highs and victories, praise Jesus. Stop allowing the devil to show up and steal your joy when in reality, that means you are doing exactly what Jesus wants you to do, or the devil wouldn't be there in the first place.

Do you really want to quit when there is something so magical, so perfect waiting for you are the top of that mountain? Do you really want to know that there was so much more for you to gain letting that friend walk away? Leaving that company or job? Do you really want to not try that business life you dream of? Or to be an artist? A singer? A nurse? Why don't you stop saying you can't, stop the excuses of I am not good enough, and go live your best life. God did not make any mistakes when he made you and gave you the talents that he did. God did not mistake you for something you are not. Instead, he gave you that talent to be amazing. He gave you that talent to help others or to inspire others. I mean, I know my calling was not to be in healthcare. Anytime I see blood, I gag. I don't think the whole giving birth is beautiful, I see it as gross, but I see motherhood as beautiful and would have nasty childbirth for my kids again.

YOU CAN DO ANYTHING YOU SET YOUR MIND TO, BEAUTIFUL

I set off to Bluefield, West Virginia in May of 2011 to become a Zumba instructor. Now let me tell you, if you have never been there at dark from good ole Tennessee and gotten lost, have you really lived? I just knew I was going to die. I just knew I would not make it there. I told my friend who was driving: *This is how we die, be prepared for it!* The woods reminded me of the movie *Wrong Turn*. I was just waiting for something to jump out and me to pee my pants. I am a chicken, you must understand, I've never even seen that movie, I'd just seen the previews. We came to a dead-end and I really thought my one-year-old, myself, and my friend were done for.

But to the glory of God, we came upon a general store. Now in the South, these are normal Ma and Pop shops. They were nice and told us that, yes, we were lost and how to get back to the main road. We finally arrived after ten, which was way past my bedtime. As we walked to the elevator, my wonderful son yells let's go swimming as he points to the dark pool. I just remember telling my friend I was not going to make it through the certification I was too tired.

Well, we did make it and obviously did not die. But I walked into this studio with all the ladies so confident and so beautiful, and I almost pooped myself, literally. I had no idea what I was getting myself into or where it would take me six years later. I had only taken a handful of classes, but I always think I can do anything I set my mind to, so I paid my fee and signed up, not knowing I didn't have a salsa booty. It was all club and booty shaking.

I only decided to do fitness because I had danced my whole life being a cheerleader. As a single mom, I thought this would be a fun, good way to earn extra money. But let's be honest. I was already working two jobs and was a full-time student in education. So, this was probably too much for me to add on, but you will learn if I think I can do it, I will do it. And truly this day was the best day into a career I had no idea would happen.

I learned so much. I learned that I hate being picked to be upfront and being required to make up a dance on the spot. I learned that I totally could not move like the master trainers could. But I learned that I love the idea of dancing and helping ladies lose weight.

What I did not know that while taking this certification was that I would be setting the path for the adventure that would help me find my passion, and that would lead me to have my own company and business. Zumba is beautiful and fun if you can salsa. You know those girls that look like they have had way too many shots and jerking their bodies around to the beat, but really they look like a chicken with their head cut off and maybe they are having an out of body experience? This was basically me, but if you need a good laugh, just think of this 130-pound white girl with no beat and truly on the verge of tears.

I did get my certifications that day. After I finished, we went to McDonald's, and I ordered me a twenty-piece chicken nugget and ate the whole dang thing and was proud. I didn't expect my friend to look at me in disgust, and I wasn't ashamed of my eating a whole chicken in ten minutes that day.

Three weeks later, I would teach my first class with two people—two friends who felt bad and came. But it was two friends who believed in me and thought this small-town girl in a rundown rec center could do something big with her dreams. In 2011, I set my first goal about what I would do with my fitness life. I gave myself until thirty to own my own studio. Did this dream happen? Let's find out.

KNOW YOUR WORTH, AND ADD TAX

*O*ver the last six years, I have gone to countless certifications, and I have been a master trainer. I finally, yes, finally, passed my personal training certification. (Have I mentioned I hate tests) and I would leave a company I swore I would be with until I die. I would find my worth. Find I truly am good enough, even if I was told my first year to quit, and that I was terrible. I would have over five thousand ladies lose hundreds of pounds a year. And I would say I made it. I did not write all this to brag. I wrote this to tell you a girl from a small town, who barely got through high school, a girl who never made a 19 on her ACT, a girl who struggles to read, a girl who was told she cannot write a paper, that if that girl can make it, if that girl can do anything she sets her mind to, so can you.

I was not the smart girl or the girl that good grades came easily to. I was not the girl who studied, which is probably why I barely passed school. I was the baby of three children, and with an older sister two grades above me who was smart, beautiful, in every club, a cheerleader, and basically perfect in my mind, I had a big shadow to fill, and I was nowhere close to filling it. But the thing is, you must have a drive. Be determined that even if you fail, you tried. And will try again. You must find your reason that you want it so bad and never quit trying. You must discover what sets your soul on fire.

I could take all the negative and bad things that happened to me that the devil tried to ruin my joy with, that I thought defined me, and I overcame them. I am not a rape victim. I am a survivor. I am not a girl who has an eating disorder. I work daily to love my body and flaws while working on the things I truly don't like. I am not the trainer who was told I would never make it without a big name company behind me. I am my own company, and I am doing this with my whole heart and with God leading me. Instead, I praise Jesus. He did not let me kill myself the many times I tried. And he gave me a story and gave me a voice to tell every lady that walks through my doors that they are worth it. They are beautiful.

You do not have to have a past like mine to make a difference in the world. You must just be willing to take the first step. And each day, take another step until you are moving along the path that God intended for you. You do not have to let one night, one moment, one bad choice, define who you are.

I hear ladies tell me weekly: *I regret this happen.* Listen, beautiful, I could regret a lot of dumb things I did or the choices I made because, in my mind, I was being *loved,* but instead, I was just being used. I do not regret those. A lot of people regret everything. It takes trauma to learn and to grow stronger and learn from the past. Your past made you the girl you are today. It is not by random chance that you are reading these words. It is no accident that this book was there for you to read. Let that past go. Let those hurtful words, hurt feelings, and mistakes go. You can't change them. You can't undo them, and you cannot go back and rewrite a wrong. All you can do is look to today and tomorrow and keep going and try not to repeat the same mistakes. Have your guard up and don't allow the same terrible things to happen. Each day is a day to know your worth and not let a moment define it. They made me who I am. I can relate to many ladies with many different backgrounds. I can relate to those who fight depression, and I can be open about it. I can relate to those who struggle with the scale and their body image. I understand that there are moments we all hide and will fear to bring our feelings and shortcomings to the surface, and that's okay.

Beautiful, you are not your past. You are not who others say you are. You are not the lies, the gossip, or even the skeletons in your closet. You are beautiful, strong, and worth so much more than a moment of regret.

So, know your worth and add tax <3

ABOUT

KALEN JOHNSON ARNOLD

Boy mom, wife, and taco lover. I grew up in a cookie-cutter family of five. Where mental health hit me hard, and life has a way of helping you use your voice to help others. Helping others learn that not being okay is okay while helping empower ladies.

Find Kalen On The Web:

www.ladyfitstudio.com

Or On Social Media:

facebook.com/kalenladyfit

instagram.com/kalenarnold

youtube.com/UCroj6O04fERQMey15IfRZrg

CPSIA information can be obtained
at www.ICGtesting.com
Printed in the USA
LVHW080230160520
655580LV00005B/1051